Greater Than a Tourist Book Series
Reviews from Readers

I think the series is wonderful and beneficial for tourists to get information before visiting the city.

-Seckin Zumbul, Izmir Turkey

I am a world traveler who has read many trip guides but this one really made a difference for me. I would call it a heartfelt creation of a local guide expert instead of just a guide.

-Susy, Isla Holbox, Mexico

New to the area like me, this is a must have!

 -Joe, Bloomington, USA

This is a good series that gets down to it when looking for things to do at your destination without having to read a novel for just a few ideas.

-Rachel, Monterey, USA

Good information to have to plan my trip to this destination.

-Pennie Farrell, Mexico

Great ideas for a port day.

-Mary Martin USA

Aptly titled, you won't just be a tourist after reading this book. You'll be greater than a tourist!

-Alan Warner, Grand Rapids, USA

Even though I only have three days to spend in San Miguel in an upcoming visit, I will use the author's suggestions to guide some of my time there. An easy read - with chapters named to guide me in directions I want to go.

 -Robert Catapano, USA

Great insights from a local perspective! Useful information and a very good value!

 -Sarah, USA

This series provides an in-depth experience through the eyes of a local. Reading these series will help you to travel the city in with confidence and it'll make your journey a unique one.

-Andrew Teoh, Ipoh, Malaysia

GREATER THAN A TOURIST- NORTH DAKOTA USA

50 Travel Tips from a Local

Rachel Reko

>TOURIST

50 TRAVEL TIPS FROM A LOCAL

BOOK DESCRIPTION

With travel tips and culture in our guidebooks written by a local, it is never too late to visit North Dakota. Greater Than a Tourist-North Dakota by Author Rachel Reko offers the inside scoop on the Roughrider State. Most travel books tell you how to travel like a tourist. Although there is nothing wrong with that, as part of the 'Greater Than a Tourist' series, this book will give you candid travel tips from someone who has lived at your next travel destination. This guide book will not tell you exact addresses or store hours but instead gives you knowledge that you may not find in other smaller print travel books. Experience cultural, culinary delights, and attractions with the guidance of a Local. Slow down and get to know the people with this invaluable guide. By the time you finish this book, you will be eager and prepared to discover new activities at your next travel destination.

Inside this travel guide book you will find:

Visitor information from a Local
Tour ideas and inspiration
Save time with valuable guidebook information

Greater Than a Tourist- A Travel Guidebook with 50 Travel Tips from a Local. Slow down, stay in one place, and get to know the people and culture. By the time you finish this book, you will be eager and prepared to travel to your next destination.

OUR STORY

Traveling is a passion of the Greater than a Tourist book series creator. Lisa studied abroad in college, and for their honeymoon Lisa and her husband toured Europe. During her travels to Malta, an older man tried to give her some advice based on his own experience living on the island since he was a young boy. She was not sure if she should talk to the stranger but was interested in his advice. When traveling to some places she was wary to talk to locals because she was afraid that they weren't being genuine. Through her travels, Lisa learned how much locals had to share with tourists. Lisa created the Greater Than a Tourist book series to help connect people with locals. A topic that locals are very passionate about sharing.

TABLE OF CONTENTS

15. Get Lost in Space

16. Drive the Lake Audubon Causeway

17. Camp Out

18. Kayak Down the River

19. Take a Trip to the Peace Gardens

20. Get Lost in the Sunflower Fields

21. Hike to Mineral Springs

22. Drop a Line

23. Explore the Far-Reaching History

24. Walk with the Dinosaurs

25. Fly High with the Air Museum

26. Dive into the Local Culture

27. Try the German Food When You Dine Out

28. Don't Skip Out on the Scandinavian Cuisine Either

29. Try a Favorite Local Snack

30. Head Out of This World

31. Take in a Show

32. Enjoy the Local Talent

33. See the City from a New Perspective

34. Grab a Slice

35. Find Good Eats in Downtown Fargo

36. Sample Some Local Beer

37. Get Nostalgic with Retro Video Games

38. Expand Your Drink Palette

39. Grab a Cup of Joe

DEDICATION

This book is dedicated to Torehn, who helped me see the beauty of our home.

ABOUT THE AUTHOR

Rachel Reko is a writer, student, and local to North Dakota twice over. Born in Arizona and raised in North Dakota, Rachel had the unique chance to experience North Dakota as both a child and again as an adult after living away from the state for six years. Rachel lives with her dog and fiancé, while pursuing her master's degree from North Dakota State University. She loves to travel and believes the best way to make friends is to explore a new place together.

HOW TO USE THIS BOOK

The *Greater Than a Tourist* book series was written by someone who has lived in an area for over three months. The goal of this book is to help travelers either dream or experience different locations by providing opinions from a local. The author has made suggestions based on their own experiences. Please check before traveling to the area in case the suggested places are unavailable.

Travel Advisories: As a first step in planning any trip abroad, check the Travel Advisories for your intended destination.
https://travel.state.gov/content/travel/en/traveladvisories/traveladvisories.html

FROM THE PUBLISHER

Traveling can be one of the most important parts of a person's life. The anticipation and memories that you have are some of the best. As a publisher of the Greater Than a Tourist, as well as the popular *50 Things to Know* book series, we strive to help you learn about new places, spark your imagination, and inspire you. Wherever you are and whatever you do I wish you safe, fun, and inspiring travel.

Lisa Rusczyk Ed. D.
CZYK Publishing

WELCOME TO
> TOURIST

View of western North Dakota

Theodore Roosevelt National Park, North Dakota

11

Sunflowers in Traill County, North Dakota

North Dakota State Capitol in Bismarck, North Dakota

*"Once a year, go someplace
you've never been before."*

Nouth Dakota is a hidden gem vacation spot,
any time of year, despite being written off
for years as one of the Midwest's
quintessential "flyover states." As a North Dakotan
twice over, I feel confident saying this reputation is
undeserved. North Dakota is a wonderful, interesting
state with small town culture and bigger city spots, as
well as thriving cultural heritage that is only growing
more diverse every year.

If you're looking to enjoy your winter, North Dakota
is a premier spot for skiing, snowboarding, and ice
skating. Take in a hockey game and get competitive
with a snowball fight. Experience the best way to sled
with inner tube sledding in Bottineau, which is my
all-time favorite winter activity. If your travels bring
you here during the summer, the rolling fields of
sunflowers, national and state parks, and historical
sites will be here to show you life on the prairie, then
and now. You'll find thriving cities like Fargo and
Bismarck or small-town experiences in places like
Regent or Anamoose. No matter your vacation
preferences, North Dakota, lovingly referred to as
"Nodak" by locals, is a too-often missed travel
destination that belongs on the top of your list.

North Dakota
United States

Bismarck North Dakota Climate

	High	Low
January	23	4
February	24	4
March	39	17
April	53	29
May	66	42
June	75	53
July	82	58
August	80	56
September	72	47
October	56	34
November	41	20
December	24	7

GreaterThanaTourist.com

Temperatures are in Fahrenheit degrees.
Source: NOAA

1. EXPLORE THE FILM HISTORY

Although it wasn't filmed here, you'll find tributes to the 1996 classic Fargo all around town. You can check out a statue of Marge Gunderson at the historic Fargo Theatre downtown, while also taking in a show. The actual prop woodchipper used in the movie lives at the Fargo-Moorhead Visitors Center, so you can swing by and snap a picture while the staff give you even more tips on Fargo's attractions and dining.

To hear any of the film's classic lines or distinctive accent, all you need to do is talk to the locals. The accent tends to be a little more pronounced in the older generations and lifelong North Dakotans, but you're just as likely to hear the younger locals utter, "Ope, let me just sneak right past ya."

2. CELEBRATE THE STATE'S DIVERSITY

Although the resident expert on Scandinavian culture year-round, the Hjemkomst Center and the Historical and Cultural Society of Clay County play host to the annual Pangea Multicultural Festival each November, a celebration of the increasingly diverse cultural makeup of Fargo-Moorhead's locals. Immerse yourself in the vibrant cultural heritage of the community's residents, including authentic food, music, arts and crafts, and storytelling. The festival hosts child-specific activities so definitely bring your children along. You can also peruse the Hjemkomst Center's current exhibitions and iconic, fully reconstructed Viking ship (more on that later), so you can learn as you enjoy the rich diversity of Fargo's communities.

3. EMBRACE THE WINTER...

If you visit Nodak anytime from November through April, I can almost guarantee you'll see snow. Even October and May have been known to see some flurries; therefore, I encourage you not to be afraid of the snow but, rather, to welcome it. I have to encourage that because otherwise you'll drive yourself crazy bemoaning the frozen tundra in which you've found yourself. But it's not just that I have to. I want you to embrace the winter in Nodak because it was one of my absolute favorite things about growing up there. As a child, I knew one of the best things in the world was putting on all my gear and sledding down a hill or building a snow fort and engaging in an epic snowball fight with my friends and sisters. At some point growing up, we all decided that rather than reveling in the fun of the snow, we would hate the cold enough that we forgot our childhood joy. But no longer.

If you keep flipping through this book, you'll find my tips on the best places to ski, snowboard, or tube, but do yourself a favor and enjoy the mounds of snow, whether you have lots of snow where you're from or not. Wherever you are in the state, find a park or public space and have a snowball fight, build your very own Frosty or Olaf, or sled down one of the many hills or dikes in town. Leave your misconceptions about winter at home and just have some fun, Jack Frost-style.

4. BUT COME PREPARED

Although North Dakota technically has four seasons, there are really only two, since you're unlikely to escape the snow in either spring or fall; therefore, I've catered many of my tips toward either winter or summer, since those are the two distinct seasons for North Dakota. Several of the events I highlight do take place in traditionally "fall" or "spring" months, but come prepared and bring winter gear even during

19

those "transition" months between North Dakota's two real seasons.

There is so much joy in snow, but frostbite is also very real. Enjoy your time in the frozen north, but don't forget your coat, gloves (or mittens), hat, scarf, boots, maybe even snow pants, if you plan on spending extensive time in deep snow. Bring the proper winter gear so you can delight in the winter but also return home with all of your current fingers and toes intact.

5. IF YOU'RE DRIVING, PACK AN EMERGENCY KIT

If you're from a state with winters like North Dakota's, you might be able to skip this particular tip. If you're unfamiliar with the type of winter where snow and ice cover every conceivable surface (roads, vegetation, cars, people, nose hairs) or maybe it's just been a while since your last experience, I cannot stress enough the necessity of an emergency kit in your car.

Pack enough blankets for your entire family, substantial (and non-perishable) snacks (think granola bars), a shovel to dig your tires out, jumper cables, a candle-powered heater, a flashlight, a first aid kit, a small bag of kitty litter, and (if you're not already wearing them) coats, hats, and gloves. You never know when you might get stuck in the snow somewhere or for how long, and kitty litter can be used to melt ice and gain traction on the snow. I was once stranded on a highway in South Dakota for 3 hours during a blizzard and stayed semi-comfortable only because my mom had already grilled me on the need for an emergency kit, so I was prepared. If you're staying exclusively in one of the bigger cities, odds are you won't have to wait that long for a tow or some help. You might be surprised, nonetheless, at how quickly you become uncomfortable, especially if you have to turn your car off, or you wind up stuck inside a snowbank. Enjoy the winter, but give it the respect it deserves and be prepared for the worst the season has to offer.

6. CHILL OUT AT THE FROSTIVAL

Fargo hosts its annual, six-week winter festival, Frostival, every January and February. Play some winter kickball, show off your impressive facial grooming in the beard contest, compete in a cardboard sled race, or drop your pants and race to victory in the Undie Run. The Frostival always

21

reminds me how excited I was, as a child, watching the snow fall and imagining the endless possibilities presented by such a blank canvas. Even if you don't compete, I highly recommend checking out the Snow Sculpture Contest, as it's truly incredible what these artists can create with snow. The Frostival team comes up with new and exciting events every year, so even if you've been to the winter festival before, go again and see what's new and/or experience your classic favorites. With something for everyone, and events spread across six weekends, Fargo's Frostival is more than worth your time.

7. ENJOY SOME WINTER SPORTS

If you're looking for some more intense winter fun, head to any of the three ski lodges in North Dakota: Huff Hills, Bottineau Winter Park, or Frost Fire Park. Huff Hills and Bottineau Winter Park both have beginner areas, if you're new to the sport, or you're like me and are a little too clumsy for serious skiing. Frost Fire Park offers group lessons, as well, if you're more comfortable learning with a group of newbies. My frequent winter spot, Huff Hills has a lodge that serves food (and beer), so you can relax between bouts on the slopes. They also host super fun events, like the annual pond skim at the end of the season or the night jam, where the staff cranks up some tunes and floodlights so you can have a new experience on the hills. Whatever your experience or wherever your travels take you, there's a spot where you can enjoy what I like to call "skilled hill gliding" in a safe (or more daring) environment.

8. EXPERIENCE THE BEST WAY TO SLED

Although you can generally find a sledding hill occupied by local children in any town in North Dakota, the best way to sled is actually on inner tubes down some serious hills. Alongside skiing and snowboarding, Bottineau Winter Park offers tubing as well. The park's staff can teach you to ski if that's what you're looking for, but tubing is all the thrill of skiing without the need for lessons or expensive equipment and the fun of sledding without needing to hike back up the hill. The winter resort will rent you the equipment for a couple hours, so you don't need to bring your own equipment, except for your winter gear. This activity really is fun for the whole family or for a group of friends, as you never get too old to enjoy a little sledding. I highly recommend you give tubing down the hills a shot, as it really is all fun with very few downsides. You may even get fast enough to feel like you're flying, if just for a moment.

9. TRY YOUR HAND AT ICE SKATING

You just cannot beat North Dakota hockey, so it should come as no surprise that rinks, both indoor and outdoor, aren't hard to come by. Most of the bigger cities will have some indoor rinks available year-round for public use during certain times of the day, so no matter when you visit, you can enjoy some time on the ice. If your visit coincides with the winter months, many public parks have outdoor rinks you can use for free, with the understanding that generally you have to bring your own skates. Ice skating is good fun for a family, or a great date idea. Additionally, many of the indoor rinks will have snacks and beverages available for purchase, so you can curl up with a hot chocolate between spins on the ice. Even if you're not the best skater, gliding across the ice while music streams in over the speakers is a great time.

10. VISIT MEDORA

Nestled in the Badlands of western Nodak, Medora cites Theodore Roosevelt with its inspiration but the North Dakota prairie town as its backdrop. The little town now possesses an impressive line-up of shows, museums, and attractions, centered primarily on life in the Roughrider State for Teddy Roosevelt and his cowboy compatriots. With a children's park, skilled re-enactors, and a pitchfork steak fondue (which is exactly as weird and fun as it sounds), Medora has a little something for everyone. If you want to spend more than a day (because, trust me, you can't see all of Medora's sites in a day), you can spend the night in the Rough Riders Hotel in downtown Medora, which, incidentally, also houses the largest library of books on and by Teddy Roosevelt. The hotel offers both modern and historic-style rooms and suites, so you can press pause on the cowboy lifestyle or embrace it wholeheartedly. Once the sun sets, you can settle in for a performance of the iconic Medora Musical. Take a step back in time and experience life in North Dakota at the turn of the 20th century, with a little added flair.

11. TREAT YOURSELF TO SOME RUSHMORE MOUNTAIN TAFFY

If you go to Medora, you absolutely must check out Rushmore Mountain Taffy, the local saltwater taffy shop. Every time I go through or to western North Dakota, I make a special stop just for taffy so tasty I had to make a separate tip just to highlight it. The little shop boasts a staggering number of flavors, but if you swing by, you absolutely must try the huckleberry taffy, a crowd favorite for North Dakotans. Parts of Medora's cowboy town are open only during tourist season (in the summer), but the taffy shop is open year-round and is willing to ship their delicious goods internationally, just in case you get hooked on the taffy after your visit. Saltwater taffy has a pretty long shelf life, so don't be afraid to grab a little of each flavor for your journey home.

12. INDULGE YOUR INNER PIONEER

If you're looking for a peek at prairie life but aren't headed all the way west to Medora, Bonanzaville in

West Fargo might be for you. Owned and operated entirely by locals, Bonanzaville is home to a real-life pioneer village and several museums, so you can learn what life was like for the early settlers of North Dakota as you walk through the life-size town and converse with re-enactors. If you check their website around the time of your visit, the Pioneer Village often hosts events, including life-size cowboy CLUE and ghost tours, so you might find something to spice up your visit even further

Lighting off fireworks within Fargo's city limits is illegal, so I would check out Bonanzaville's incredible Fourth of July celebration if you're in town for the 4th. Their celebration includes a parade, games, and fair food, ending with a spectacular firework display over the fairgrounds. I have been to their annual party more than once, in part because their team of volunteers puts on an excellent event and in part because the pioneer village is just good fun, even if it isn't the Fourth of July. Bonanzaville is a great way to take a peek into the past and understand how the past influences the present and future.

13. ENJOY THE NATURAL BEAUTY BUT RESPECT THE WILDLIFE

Named in honor of the president who founded the United States Forest Service to protect wildlife and public lands, Theodore Roosevelt National Park will satisfy the nature enthusiast in you. The northern section of the park is home to the park's most iconic view, River Bend Overlook. Rangers are available in the southern section to guide you through some of the park's activities, including my personal favorite, the full-moon walk. I know it requires you to stay up a little late, but seeing the park through the moonlight shines an ethereal light over nature's beauty and makes you see the entire park from a new perspective. If your stop in the park can't be extensive, stop at the Painted Canyon Visitors Center in the southern unit of the park. You can catch the view of Painted Canyon, and maybe even spot some bison, without needing to make a full excursion into the park.

If you have the time, however, I wholeheartedly encourage you to really take your time. The park offers many campsites, trails, and opportunities to view the native wildlife, including mule deer, prairie dogs, coyotes, eagles, elk, and, of course, bison. You don't fully comprehend the majesty, and the size, of the bison until they're standing 100 feet from you, but make sure you give the wildlife a wide berth. The animals, like many creatures, don't take too kindly to people in their territory, and the bison, in particular, can pose a serious threat if you get too close. Enjoy the sight of the animals in their natural habitat, just don't get too close.

14. BRING A COMFY BLANKET AND SETTLE IN FOR THE NIGHT.

Theodore Roosevelt National Park also happens to be a good distance from the nearest city, making the view of the night sky particularly stunning for amateur stargazers and seasoned astronomers alike. Although both park units have viewing areas on top of natural plateaus perfect for viewing the night sky, the northern section is just a bit further away from Dickinson, making the view just a bit more stunning from that vantage point. Bring a comfy blanket (or two), a thermos of your favorite drink, and spend a night gazing at the beauty of the sky beyond planet Earth. Telescope recommended, but not required.

15. GET LOST IN SPACE

If you're looking for a more guided glance into the galaxy, the Dakota Nights Astronomy Festival takes place late August to early September in and around Theodore Roosevelt National Park and Medora. The three-day festival hosts kids' activities and crafts, a rocket construction and launch event, and more. Go on a solar system hike, where you start at the sun and hike your way to Neptune (Pluto, we'll never forget you), so you can learn about our solar system as you get in a light nature hike. Astronomers will even set up telescopes so you can safely view a sunspot. Learn about the great big universe out there while taking in the surreal beauty of outer space through telescopes positioned by astronomers to give you a glimpse of the night sky that inspired and perplexed countless civilizations before us.

16. DRIVE THE LAKE AUDUBON CAUSEWAY

If you find yourself near Lake Audubon and/or Lake Sakakawea, do yourself a favor and drive down the Lake Audubon Causeway between the two lakes. I won't try to describe it here, but I will say it's one of the coolest sights in North Dakota. The Midwestern version of a bridge connecting an island to the mainland, the only disappointing thing is how short the strip of road is. Rest assured, though, you can drive over it as many times as you'd like.

17. CAMP OUT

Frequent visits to my great uncle's cabin near Washburn, along the Missouri River, gave me a strong attachment to the forests and shores of the Missouri. There are many camping grounds throughout North Dakota, on lakes and on rivers, but I particularly urge you to camp out in western/central North Dakota.

With miles of hiking trails winding through the Badlands, Little Missouri State Park has limited camping sites but offers both primitive and modern sites, for a variety of camping styles. Lake Sakakawea State Park offers two cabins, if camping in a tent or RV isn't your style. The park also has modern, primitive, and group campsites, so you can bring all your friends camping with you. More heavily developed than the more natural Little Missouri State Park, Lake Sakakawea State Park also features a full-service marina, playgrounds, and prime fishing locations. My personal favorite camping site in all of North Dakota is Cross Ranch State Park, as it is the only campsite I've been to myself that is right alongside the Missouri River. Cabins and yurts are available to rent, if you don't have access to your own camping gear, as are modern, primitive, and group campsites. While Lake Sakakawea State Park rests along the shores of the lake, Cross Ranch State Park is nestled right alongside the roaring Missouri River and features a boat ramp and several picturesque hiking trails.

18. KAYAK DOWN THE RIVER

If you stay along the Missouri, you must take a kayak (or canoe, if you're more of a team sport person) down the river. You can rent one from Cross Ranch State Park, Missouri Kayak Adventures, or Paddle On North Dakota. Several of the rental places offer paddleboards as well, if that's more your interest. See the magnificence of the surrounding land as the Missouri cuts through, while also getting in a nice workout. You might even get a sense of what Lewis and Clark may have experienced during their travels down the river in the early-19th century. A few words of caution: first, bring more beer than you think you need, in case you get stuck on a sandbar. Second, although this activity is exciting and more than worthwhile, bear in mind that the Missouri is a large and occasionally fast-flowing river. The kind of windy days common across the Great Plains can, at times, whip the river into waves that could easily swamp a kayak or canoe. Finally, you may encounter obstacles along your journey, including sandbars or uprooted trees at the bottom of the river, so pay attention to the water, know your paddling ability, and don't try to push it. The river is deep and wide, so there's plenty of space to enjoy yourself, as long as you remember to pay attention and be careful.

19. TAKE A TRIP TO THE PEACE GARDENS

The Peace Gardens, along the North Dakota-Canadian border, are breathtaking in the summer for those willing to brave the pollen. The blooming season is a bit different every year, but you're generally safe to go after the snow has all melted into August or September. Although the Formal Garden is the crowning jewel of the Peace Gardens, don't stop your trip there. Make sure you leave time to take in the hiking trails, wildflower fields, and manmade waterfalls, as well as the many facilities of the Formal Garden beyond the flowers, including the reflecting pool, Peace Chapel, and the Carillon Bell Tower. If you're looking to spend more time, the grounds of the Peace Gardens also host two freshwater lakes and camping facilities, so you can camp out and enjoy the gardens the next day too. I've never spent less than a half day at the Peace Gardens, so make sure you give yourself enough time explore the site, if you're going for the first, or honestly even the fifth time.

20. GET LOST IN THE SUNFLOWER FIELDS

A little-known fact, North Dakota is one of the nation's top sunflower producers, so the state is teeming with fields of the beautiful blooms. Although the fields growing the flowers changes year-to-year, you can check out North Dakota Tourism's website to find the best spots for sunflower scouting in any given year. Growing season generally peaks in mid-August, so all you have to do is drive around western or central North Dakota to find yourself lost among the flowers. It's a perfect picture opportunity and a way to appreciate the rarely explored beauty of the state.

21. HIKE TO MINERAL SPRINGS

North Dakota's only natural waterfall is hidden along a hiking trail in Sheyenne River State Forest. Called the Mineral Springs Waterfall, this little natural wonder is one of North Dakota's best kept secrets, as the land across much of the state seems too flat to support a waterfall. There is a marked trail, easy to find and easy to walk for all ages, to lead you to the waterfall. The trail is open to dogs, as well, as long as you keep them leashed, so you don't have to leave your dog at home to enjoy the sights of the park. Just don't spend so much time looking for the underground spring feeding into the waterfall that you miss the view of the incredible wildlife surrounding you. The forest along the way offers spectacular views of the Sheyenne River Valley, so take your time and enjoy the view.

22. DROP A LINE

Whether you're an avid angler or a casual fisherman, North Dakota has plenty of spots to stop for a while and drop in a line. Devils Lake and Lake Sakakawea are both particularly great spots, although any of the lakes around you will do just fine for an afternoon (or early morning) on the water. If you're visiting in the winter and looking to try your hand at ice fishing, Devils Lake is known for its excellent ice fishing, as the lake is huge and fully stocked with walleye, perch, and good-sized pike. You can stay at any of the modern hotels around the lake, or head to a lodge like Woodland Resort, which boasts a bait shop, fish-cleaning station, and guide services, alongside their hotel accommodations.

If you're looking to try your hand at catching the local favorite walleye, head to Lake Sakakawea and grab some worms, leeches, or minnows. You'll need a boat, trolling at a low speed, if you hope to catch some of these fish, so bring yours or find a marina where you can rent one. The stretch of river referred to as "central Missouri River" is also renowned for its walleye fishing, as well as Chinook salmon and various species of trout, so the odds are pretty good you'll catch something worthwhile here.

23. EXPLORE THE FAR-REACHING HISTORY

The North Dakota Heritage Center and Museum explores North Dakota's rich history, starting at the age of dinosaurs, when North Dakota was covered by oceans and populated by sea creatures. The museum continues through the ice age, exploring the terrestrial life in North Dakota and the state's evolving ecosystems. Continuing into the life of both early and contemporary North Dakotan peoples, the exhibits feature pottery and beadwork, as well as a firsthand perspective on farming and hunting in North Dakota. The Governors Gallery also features a traveling exhibit from nationally renowned museums, like the Smithsonian Institutes, so you can see exhibits not specifically related to North Dakota as well. Take a break at the museum store or James River Café, then keep exploring some of their interactive exhibits. With a Tyrannosaurus skeleton cast to the world's largest giant squid fossil, this museum in Bismarck explores life in Nodak from the age of dinosaurs until the 21st century, so it's sure to have something for every type of history buff.

24. WALK WITH THE DINOSAURS

The Badlands Dinosaur Museum in Dickinson features an expanding exhibit of fossils and minerals millions of years old. Renovated in 2015, the museum is still installing new exhibits and preparing new fossils in their on-site laboratory that is open to the public for viewings. Much of the museum's proceeds are put toward their research and fieldwork programs, as they continue expanding their collection and excavating the fossil beds in North Dakota's badlands. Although not the flashiest dinosaur museum you've ever seen, this local gem is more than worth your time, especially since it will teach you quite a bit about the science of paleontology, excavation, and preservation across North Dakota and the money you spend is put toward continued science education.

25. FLY HIGH WITH THE AIR MUSEUM

Between the modern reconnaissance drones and an incredibly accurate re-creation of the Wright Brothers' flyer, the Fargo Air Museum is a must see for history buffs, aviation enthusiasts, and casual fans of the miracle of flight. If you hang around the museum long enough, you may even see a number of the airplanes, even the older ones, take flight, a distinctly unique experience among air museums. There are guided tours available if you'd like a little more information about the rotating exhibits as you walk through, but you're also welcome to stroll at your own pace. Also, the Air Museum in Fargo is pet-friendly and hosts fun and educational events, so you can encourage your kids to learn without having to leave the dog alone in the hotel room. The Air Museum is right down the road from Hector International Airport in Fargo, so you can make it your first or last stop in town, if that's most convenient for you.

26. DIVE INTO THE LOCAL CULTURE

Many of North Dakota's locals, myself included, boast heritage from Scandinavian nations, and the culture of the state most clearly reflects that during local Viking festivals. In June, the Fargo-Moorhead community hosts the Midwest Viking Festival around town, centered on the Hjemkomst Center in Moorhead. You can shop for Scandinavian goods and foods while listening to Viking storytellers and musicians. The Viking Village gives you a taste of life in a Viking settlement, including games, contests, artisans, and a battle re-enactment.

If you're checking out the local Scandinavian culture, you must head to the Hjemkomst Center at some point and take in the glory of the museum's full-scale replica of the Gokstad Viking ship and used as a burial ship for Vikings in the ninth century. Although a replica, this ship has actually sailed to Norway and back, but I'll let the museum tell you that particularly fascinating family tale.

If your travels bring you a little further west, but you're still interested in checking out some Scandinavian culture, Norsk Høstfest in Minot will scratch that itch for you. Boasting authentic Scandinavian food, music, and goods, either festival

will give you the chance to experience the heritage of
North Dakota's locals for yourself.

27. TRY THE GERMAN FOOD WHEN YOU DINE OUT

Many longtime residents of North Dakota claim roots
in not just Scandinavian cultures but in German
cultures as well. Many of the delectable delights have
made their way to North Dakotan restaurants from
Europe. Try a taste with local favorite knoephla soup
at Kroll's Diner, CJ's Kitchen, or Rising Bread Co.
I'll admit that I am a bit of a bad local in one regard: I
was skeptical about knoephla soup for a long time but
tried it again as an adult. I've been kicking myself
ever since for the years I lived in North Dakota
without eating knoephla soup. If you're not interested
in the dumpling soup (or have had it before and are
looking for something different), Würst Bier Hall
offers a taste of Bavarian pretzels and German
American würst, much of it from North Dakotan
towns. Fargo also hosts an annual German Folk
Festival in the summer, so there are plenty of chances
to try some authentic kuchen. Although these
restaurants are all found in Fargo, many towns across
the state feature their own German-based local spots,

so all you need to do is ask a local, and they'll be able to recommend something to you.

28. DON'T SKIP OUT ON THE SCANDINAVIAN CUISINE EITHER

Although this is a little harder to find than the German delights, it isn't any less worthwhile to try. Local churches will often host "lutefisk dinners" where you can try the namesake food, amongst other Scandinavian offerings. If your travels take you to Fargo, Freddy's Lefse Bakery has perfected the traditional flat potato treat. With a retail shop in West Fargo, you can try lefse, made fresh daily by their seasoned bakers. Sons of Norway in downtown Fargo is open for lunch and generally offers Norwegian specials alongside American fare. Any of the Viking festivals throughout the state will also offer food you've likely never tried, so no matter where you go, follow the scent of the lutefisk and go from there.

29. TRY A FAVORITE LOCAL SNACK

Dot's Pretzels developed their distinctive pretzel recipe from a family recipe made in Dot's kitchen for years. Now, the brand boasts bakeries in several states, but you need to try the original salty snack during your time in North Dakota. Most of the grocery stores (and many convenience stores) throughout the state sell the local fave, as does the goods store in Hector International Airport, so you can snag a bag (or four) on your way out of the state. You should also check out their website for some killer recipes using Dot's Pretzels, so you can expand your recipe repertoire with Dot's homemade pretzels.

30. HEAD OUT OF THIS WORLD

If you're looking for a fun way to feed your kids and work off some of their energy simultaneously, look no further than local chain restaurant Space Aliens. With locations in Fargo, Grand Forks, Bismarck, and Minot, you can try this favorite of local children no matter where in the state your travels take you. Try the Martian Munchies or their famous ribs, then let loose on their huge arcade.

43

Win enough tickets and you can take home a nice prize, but even if you don't win that many, you can still have fun playing with friends and family. Since you're almost guaranteed to have fun, make sure you stop by the merch stand up front and get a t-shirt or alien cup to mark your time there. Parents, don't worry: each location also has a full-service bar to keep you entertained while your kids spend hours in the arcade.

31. TAKE IN A SHOW

The theater scene in Fargo is teeming with local talent, so I highly recommend checking out a show, if your dates match up. There are plenty of local troupes, so your odds of catching a show are pretty good. Both Trollwood Performing Arts School's and Fargo-Moorhead Community Theater's productions are incredibly well done. Trollwood Performing Arts School also often host events at the Bluestem Center for the Arts with vocal and theatrical performances as well as arts, crafts, and vendors. If you have a chance, be sure to buy tickets to their latest offering. Minnesota State University in Moorhead and North Dakota State University both boasts fantastic theater programs that, in my experience, produce amazing shows, so if you have the chance to check out a production, it is more than worth your time.

32. ENJOY THE LOCAL TALENT

It would be impossible to namecheck all the great local bands and performers, or the venues they occupy, so here's just a small sampling of the places you should go to find local musicians. You can find rock bands, pop singers, country crooners, or alternative rockers in countless restaurants and bars in Fargo on the weekends, especially during the summer months. I recommend, in particular, checking out local musicians at the Aquarium above Dempsey's Pub, the Spirits Lounge and Casino inside the Holiday Inn, or Lucky 13's Pub on weekend nights. Each venue has their own distinct atmosphere, but all three are known to frequently host some of the best musicians in town. The bartenders are great, the drinks are cold, and the music is rocking.

33. SEE THE CITY FROM A NEW PERSPECTIVE

The rooftop patio at the Hodo Lounge offers a whole new way to see Fargo's thriving downtown, with great drinks and good food while you're at it. The cozy patio is teeming with greenery, so you still feel grounded as you sit above the street and watch the city buzz below you. You might even catch a glimpse of the illusive Fargo Spaceman (@fargospaceman on Instagram or Facebook) in the midst of a downtown photoshoot. Try the local favorite bison burger and sip a cool beverage in the summer heat. Make sure you check the weather before you go, though, because the patio can be a bit unpleasant if the prairie winds are blowing a bit too hard. The ambiance of the rooftop patio is perfect for an evening dinner with your special someone or happy hour with friends.

34. GRAB A SLICE

If you're wanting a slice of gooey, cheesy pizza, search out one of the locally owned stores or chains to satisfy your craving. If you're in Fargo or just a bit north in Grand Forks, check out Rhombus Guys for inventive pizza and locally brewed beer. Their selection of both is huge, so they're sure to have something you'll love. If beer isn't your thing, they also have a sizable (and creative) cocktail list to enjoy. Many of Fargo's bigger cities sport a Spicy Pie pizza shop, a local chain of pizzeria's whose slices are just big enough to fold, Brooklyn-style. They serve whole pizzas or by the slice, but you can also find grinders, appetizers, and dessert. They'll work with you on your dietary restrictions too, so don't be afraid to check out either restaurant, even if you're gluten-free, dairy-free, or vegan.

35. FIND GOOD EATS IN DOWNTOWN FARGO

Although you can find great local food in many locations around Fargo, the place to start is downtown. Stuffed to the brim with locally owned eateries, you can't help but stumble upon something delicious and unique. A delightful local bakery, Nichole's Fine Pastry offers sweet and savory delights along with the coziest atmosphere in town. Vinyl Taco, a local chain with locations in Fargo and Grand Forks, serves up incredible Mexican American food and a tequila selection to match. Rosey's Bistro & Bar provides the best comfort food in town with a cool bistro ambiance to match. My favorite meal after a night of revelry is Rosey's Snobby Frenchman, a twist on the classic grilled cheese with apples and walnuts for a sweet and smoky finish. From Dempsey's Pub and Twist to the Old Broadway Grill and Pounds, you'll find local food to satisfy every craving on or near Broadway in downtown Fargo.

36. SAMPLE SOME LOCAL BEER

Fargo is a hotspot for North Dakota's local breweries. Many local restaurants have beers from not just Fargo breweries but also smaller Nodak breweries on tap, so you can try a sample of North Dakota's brewery scene from all over town. Stop by any of the locally owned breweries, like Drekker or Fargo Brewing Company for your best chance at some unique and truly delicious beer.

Drekker, whose building is modeled after the Viking dining halls common throughout Scandinavian countries, is an unbeatable stop for the brew enthusiasts among you. They also sell cans of their current offerings in four packs right in the brewery. Although I'm not an IPA fan, I hear great things from my friends about Drekker's IPA selection. My favorite of their beers, though, is the People Eater, a blueberry basil sour ale named after the iconic Flying

Purple People Eaters. It's got just the right amount of sweetness and bite that I love most in a sour, and I've never had another beer with the flavor profile as the People Eater.

As for Fargo Brewing Company, they'll also sell you packs of cans in a variety of beers. Their most iconic beer is their Stone's Throw Scottish Ale, available on tap throughout the city as a crowd favorite. My personal favorite is the Kenny's Lemonade Radler, which is the absolute perfect beer for a summer night on the patio or the lake. Regardless of your tastes, Fargo breweries will have something I'm confident you'll love.

37. GET NOSTALGIC WITH RETRO VIDEO GAMES

Pixeled Brewing Co., a local brewery in downtown Fargo, boasts an impressive number of retro video games in their warehouse-turned-barcade. Enjoy some cold beer while you shoot down alien forces in Galaga, evade the food chasing you in BurgerTime, or show the ghosts who's boss with the original Pac-Man. Pixeled Brewing Co. is always expanding their selection of both beer and games, so even if you've been before, go again and check out their new additions. You can relive your childhood arcade

49

experience, but with beer this time, so really, what more can you ask for?

38. EXPAND YOUR DRINK PALETTE

Although known for its brewery scene, Fargo also boasts a few truly interesting and unique local drinkeries: Prairie Rose Meadery, Wild Terra Cider Bar, and Proof Artisan Distillery. Prairie Rose Meadery makes their award-winning traditional mead, fruit mead, and spiced mead using ingredients almost exclusively grown and harvested in North Dakota. They sell by the glass in their meadery or by the bottle in person or online, so you can take some of their delicious mead home to share (or keep for yourself).

Wild Terra Cider Bar pushes your expectations of ciders, using apples from both the Pacific Northwest and local orchards. They don't just offer cider, if that's not your thing, but I strongly urge you to give one a try. My favorite, though it unfortunately may not be in rotation during your visit, is the Ramble On, a totally unique cider with melon and banana flavors.

Proof Artisan Distillery operates on a historic site in downtown Fargo and produces award-winning spirits made almost exclusively from locally grown corn, potatoes, barley. You should visit their tasting room (open Thursday through Saturday) to enjoy their unique, handcrafted cocktails. You can also tour the distillery, take a mixology class from their seasoned bartenders, or purchase their spirits off-sale. Expand your expectations of both Fargo and alcohol by checking out any or all of these awesome places during your stay.

39. GRAB A CUP OF JOE

Although you can find national coffee chains on every corner, I recommend you skip the drive-thru in favor of coffee from a local shop like Red Raven Espresso Parlor or Atomic Coffee. Red Raven serves only organic coffee and sells a number of sweet treats to go along with a steaming cup, including their incredible donuts that are made using a generations-old family recipe.

Atomic Coffee is my favorite spot to grab a tea and a treat and settle in for some studying or casual people watching. The eco-friendly local coffee shop brews only fair-trade coffee and has a selection of vegan and vegetarian food options, so there's something for everyone. Also, the building itself is gorgeous, with an exposed pipe ceiling, featured local art, and huge windows overlooking Broadway. Either coffee shop is a great location to relax in the morning or take a midday caffeine and snack break.

40. TUCK INTO UNIQUE FAIR FOOD

The North Dakota State Fair offers the usual rides, carnival games, and animal-based competitions characteristic of state fairs, but the reason you need to check out the state fair is the food. While the vendors do offer fair staples like funnel cake and giant corn dogs, the Food Frenzy competition requires vendors to submit a novel fair food, one that has never been sold at the state fair before. The Food Frenzy judges pick a most creative and Best Bites winner in both savory and sweet categories to help you find things you've never tried before, no matter what you're craving. Come for the rides, stay for the jalapeño popper pizza, brownie waffle stick (note: actual 2019 winners), or whatever else the vendors have thought up for the competition this year.

41. CATCH A GLIMPSE OF A RARE ALBINO BUFFALO

Just west of Fargo, Jamestown's National Buffalo Museum in the Frontier Village offers the unique chance to see the world's largest bison statue while also taking in the sight of actual bison roaming the plains. The museum's wild herd includes Dakota Legend, the last living albino bison in North Dakota. White buffalo (or albino bison) are rare, occurring in just one out of every 10 million buffalo births, are considered sacred in many Great Plains tribes, including the Lakota Sioux, so don't miss your chance to take in the beautiful sight of Dakota Legend in all her majesty.

Learn about these incredible native creatures and the cultures that lived with them on North Dakota's plains in centuries past. Although once near extinction, the species has been restored and is now the national mammal of the United States. This museum also offers the chance to learn about how you can help preserve the native bison of North America's plains.

42. DRIVE THROUGH ENCHANTED COUNTRY

In between small towns Gladstone and Regent, miles from the nearest interstate, the Enchanted Highway showcases the talent and aspiration of one local artist and teacher to create something so unique it draws travelers away from the interstate and through small town Nodak. All along that 32-mile stretch of highway, artist Gary Greff has built giant metal sculptures representing life in North Dakota against a backdrop of lovely hills and pastures. You can drive along the highway (or stop for a longer look), taking in the beauty of North Dakota's prairies juxtaposed with the splendor of the artwork. At the end of the road, there's a little gift shop where you can buy some delicious ice cream and miniature versions of any sculpture that caught your eye along the way. If you're a road tripper, there is a nice RV park in Regent where you can stay overnight after your trip down the Enchanted Highway.

43. SPEND A NIGHT AT THE ENCHANTED CASTLE

At the end of the Enchanted Highway, a medieval-themed hotel rests, where you can enjoy the rare juxtaposition of small-town North Dakota and Europe in the Middle Ages. Enjoy a meal fit for a king (but perhaps named for a peasant) in the attached tavern, even if you're not a hotel guest. And if you do have the time to stay a night or two, fear not: the hotel has modern amenities to keep you comfortable, like hot tubs, a fitness center, and the ever-necessary electric lighting. Step backward in time (but not too far backward) at the Enchanted Castle in Regent, a truly charming property with the façade of a castle, complete with huge drawbridge.

44. STAND IN THE EXACT MIDDLE OF THE CONTINENT

It's a little-known fact outside of North Dakota that North America's exact geographic center is near a small town called Rugby. Although the monument has been moved a few times to accommodate construction, you can still get out and take a picture with the stone structure. You can even buy a post card at the nearby gift shop. It's a quick stop, so you definitely don't need to allot more than, say, 15 minutes, unless you'd like to sit and sip a coffee as well.

45. PUT YOUR MONEY WHERE YOUR MOUTH IS

If you're 21 or older, you can spend a day (and night) at any of the great casinos in North Dakota. Right on the border between North and South Dakota, Dakota Magic Casino is the largest casino in the state, hosting slot machines, blackjack, Texas holdem, and more, as well as world-class hotel accommodations, dining, and golf. If you time your stay correctly, you can take in a concert or performance from any number of touring acts. Prairie Knights Casino and Resort, in central North Dakota, boasts similar accommodations, if your journey is not taking you as far east as Hankinson. The Sky Dancer Casino and Resort, along the North Dakota/Canada border, is for you if you're looking for the same caliber of casino and hotel a little farther north. Stay and take in a show, maybe even play a few rounds of your game of choice, if you're feeling lucky.

46. GET SPOOKED

If you're anything like me and a new destination means a chance to seek out a local paranormal experience, then the Sage Hill Bed and Breakfast is for you. Located in Anamoose, this quaint B&B is perfect if you're looking for a quiet getaway, with a little hint of the spooky. According to a local urban legend (that may or may not be true), a superintendent and student burned to death in the school many years ago, so it could be their spirits that still linger in the hotel.

The alleged ghosts of Sage Hill are friendly but are also known to be a bit mischievous. You may find your items moved from where you left them, or disappeared altogether, although they almost always turn up before you leave. Each of the three spacious rooms is very comfortable, and the food, prepared by owners Jackie and Brad, is delicious, but keep your eyes peeled during lunch and dinner, as it's said the dining room might just be the most haunted room in the place. I myself have visited the B&B and, though none of my things seemed misplaced during my stay, I did have an inexplicable encounter. When entering or leaving my room throughout my stay, I could smell the distinctive odor of cigar smoke in the hallway, which is strange since there is a strict no-smoking policy on the property.

47. VISIT ENDANGERED ANIMALS

If you want to hang with the monkeys for an afternoon, just south of Fargo in Wahpeton, Chahinkapa Zoo is home to North Dakota's largest collection of endangered animals. Take in the sight of the rhinos playing in the mud, the grizzly bears rolling about, or any number of big cats lazing in the sun. You can book private, behind the scenes tours to get a little more up close and personal with several of the animals, including Tal the orangutan, the Australian Red Kangaroos, or Gunner and Gideon the white rhinos. Learn about how the zoo is trying to preserve endangered species through their breeding program, as you enjoy the company of many of your favorites.

If you can't make the trip to Wahpeton, Fargo's Red River Valley Zoo also features both exotic and native animals in their exhibits, but they specialize in some of the rarest cold climate species in the world. You can book encounters with the zoo's porcupines, baby camels (including feeding!), and iconic red pandas. The zoo offers both summer and winter education programs, so you and yours can learn a little more about the wonderful creatures who share the planet with us. If you're traveling with a group, look into the sleeping bag safari experience before you head to

North Dakota, so you can experience the zoo after hours, including a close-up look at the animals and a guided night hike.

48. APPRECIATE THE LOCAL ART

Right in the heart of downtown Fargo, Plains Art Museum plays host to a number of nationally renowned collections and changing exhibitions, including collections of traditional African works, modern and post-modern art, and photographs. Their particular focus, however, remains on Native artwork in all its forms, including the breathtaking paintings, photography, and sculptural beaded works of traditional and modern Native artists. They also have a regional art collection, made exclusively by Midwestern locals.

You can walk freely or schedule a tour through the museum's extensive collections. You may even have the chance to make some art yourself in one of the many classes and events scheduled at the museum. Check out the museum store for some truly exceptional artwork you can take home and/or give as gifts. I own at least four gorgeous, handblown glass ornaments I bought during trips to the museum. Plains Art Museum is an art museum with a uniquely historical undertone, as many of the resident artists work to bring their culture to life through a variety of mediums.

If you're more interested in living art, the museum launched a fairly recent enterprise to engage artists directly with local communities to create "defiant gardens." The first is the Heritage Garden and Amphitheater, just across the Red River in Moorhead, that incorporated elements of the decommissioned power plant that sits nearby into the park. The second is the Pollinator Garden, in downtown Fargo, which, in addition to acting as the home of nature-inspired sculptures, helps sustain the local populations of bees, butterflies, and hummingbirds. This garden even inspired the Museum's Buzz Lab program, which engages teens in education, creation, and advocacy that benefits our suffering populations of pollinators.

49. GET SPORTY WITH LOCAL TEAMS

Although North Dakota doesn't have any professional teams, there's no shortage of local teams to support. Fargo has a semi-professional baseball team, the RedHawks, who play at Newman Outdoor Field. At the RedHawks games, you can enjoy the summer weather with Dippin' Dots, ballpark franks, and the lively mascot Hawkeye (who, in my experience, is an expert dancer and an excellent showman). If hockey is what you're looking for in the great frozen north, you can check out a Fargo Force game or head north to Grand Forks to see the champion UND Fighting Hawks take on a competitor. For most other sports, you can check out the NDSU Bison teams. The school is particularly renowned for their football team, but make sure you go early to enjoy some morning tailgating before the game. Football isn't the only sport worth seeing, though, as the Bison basketball teams have been known to dominate their competitors as well. No matter the sport, you're sure to find a great local team to support, while you sip a beer (or soda) and munch on a giant pretzel.

50. WHEN IN DOUBT, TALK TO THE LOCALS

If you're reading this book, you've already decided you're looking for some suggestions from a local; however, I don't know everything, and certainly couldn't fit it all in fifty tips, even if I did. During your time in North Dakota, don't be afraid to ask for help, suggestions, and advice from the strangers around you. North Dakota's biggest draw is its incredibly nice people, and, coming from a longtime local, the people live up to the hype. If you get lost, ask someone for directions. If you can't figure out what to eat for lunch, ask for suggestions from your hotel clerk or Lyft driver. Ask for a dinner recommendation while you're at lunch, and your server should have some killer insights. If you don't know what to do today, you can definitely stop someone on the street and get some help or great suggestions. Take advantage of the North Dakota-nice mythos and pick the brains of the locals around you. Each community has a wealth of knowledge you'll only be given access to if you aren't afraid to talk to the locals.

TOP REASONS TO BOOK THIS TRIP

Natural Beauty: North Dakota is ripe with spectacular views of nature.

Food: The food is an amazing and unique tribute to the heritage of North Dakota's local.

North Dakota Nice: The state has a rich, local culture of kindness and compassion.

OTHER RESOURCES:

ND Tourism: https://www.ndtourism.com

Fargo-Moorhead Visitors Center: (701) 282-3653

ND Government Tourism:
https://www.nd.gov/innovation-industries/tourism

Visit the USA:
https://www.visittheusa.com/state/north-dakota

PACKING AND PLANNING TIPS

A Week before Leaving

- Arrange for someone to take care of pets and water plants.

- Email and Print important Documents.

- Get Visa and vaccines if needed.

- Check for travel warnings.

- Stop mail and newspaper.

- Notify Credit Card companies where you are going.

- Passports and photo identification is up to date.

- Pay bills.

- Copy important items and download travel Apps.

- Start collecting small bills for tips.

- Have post office hold mail while you are away.

- Check weather for the week.

- Car inspected, oil is changed, and tires have the correct pressure.

- Check airline luggage restrictions.

- Download Apps needed for your trip.

Right Before Leaving

- Contact bank and credit cards to tell them your location.

- Clean out refrigerator.

- Empty garbage cans.

- Lock windows.

- Make sure you have the proper identification with you.

- Bring cash for tips.

- Remember travel documents.

- Lock door behind you.

- Remember wallet.

- Unplug items in house and pack chargers.

- Change your thermostat settings.

- Charge electronics, and prepare camera memory cards.

READ OTHER
GREATER THAN A TOURIST
BOOKS

Greater Than a Tourist- Geneva Switzerland: 50 Travel Tips from a Local by Amalia Kartika

Greater Than a Tourist- St. Croix US Birgin Islands USA: 50 Travel Tips from a Local by Tracy Birdsall

Greater Than a Tourist- San Juan Puerto Rico: 50 Travel Tips from a Local by Melissa Tait

Greater Than a Tourist - Lake George Area New York USA: 50 Travel Tips from a Local by Janine Hirschklau

Greater Than a Tourist - Monterey California United States: 50 Travel Tips from a Local by Katie Begley

Greater Than a Tourist - Chanai Crete Greece: 50 Travel Tips from a Local by Dimitra Papagrigoraki

Greater Than a Tourist - The Garden Route Western Cape Province South Africa: 50 Travel Tips from a Local by Li-Anne McGregor van Aardt

Greater Than a Tourist - Sevilla Andalusia Spain: 50 Travel Tips from a Local by Gabi Gazon

Children's Book: *Charlie the Cavalier Travels the World* by Lisa Rusczyk Ed. D.

> TOURIST

Follow us on Instagram for beautiful travel images:

http://Instagram.com/GreaterThanATourist

Follow *Greater Than a Tourist* on Amazon.

>Tourist Podcast

>T Website

>T Youtube

>T Facebook

>T Goodreads

>T Amazon

>T Mailing List

>T Pinterest

>T Instagram

>T Twitter

>T SoundCloud

>T LinkedIn

>T Map

> TOURIST

At *Greater Than a Tourist*, we love to share travel tips with you. How did we do? What guidance do you have for how we can give you better advice for your next trip? Please send your feedback to GreaterThanaTourist@gmail.com as we continue to improve the series. We appreciate your constructive feedback. Thank you.

METRIC CONVERSIONS

TEMPERATURE

110° F —
100° F —   — 40° C
90° F —
80° F —   — 30° C
70° F —   — 20° C
60° F —
50° F —   — 10° C
40° F —
32° F —   — 0° C
20° F —
10° F —   — -10° C
0° F —   — -18° C
-10° F —
-20° F —   — -30° C

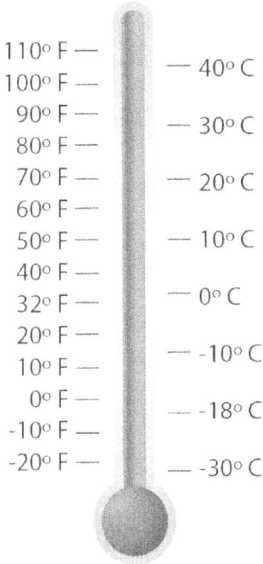

To convert F to C:

Subtract 32, and then multiply
by 5/9 or .5555.

To Convert C to F:

Multiply by 1.8
and then add 32.

32F = 0C

LIQUID VOLUME

To Convert:..................Multiply by
U.S. Gallons to Liters................ 3.8
U.S. Liters to Gallons 26
Imperial Gallons to U.S. Gallons 1.2
Imperial Gallons to Liters....... 4.55
Liters to Imperial Gallons 22
1 Liter = .26 U.S. Gallon
1 U.S. Gallon = 3.8 Liters

DISTANCE

To convert ....Multiply by
Inches to Centimeters 2.54
Centimeters to Inches 39
Feet to Meters....................... .3
Meters to Feet 3.28
Yards to Meters 91
Meters to Yards 1.09
Miles to Kilometers 1.61
Kilometers to Miles............ .62
1 Mile = 1.6 km
1 km = .62 Miles

WEIGHT

1 Ounce = .28 Grams
1 Pound = .4555 Kilograms
1 Gram = .04 Ounce
1 Kilogram = 2.2 Pounds

75

TRAVEL QUESTIONS

- Do you bring presents home to family or friends after a vacation?

- Do you get motion sick?

- Do you have a favorite billboard?

- Do you know what to do if there is a flat tire?

- Do you like a sun roof open?

- Do you like to eat in the car?

- Do you like to wear sun glasses in the car?

- Do you like toppings on your ice cream?

- Do you use public bathrooms?

- Did you bring a cell phone and does it have power?

- Do you have a form of identification with you?

- Have you ever been pulled over by a cop?

- Have you ever given money to a stranger on a road trip?

- Have you ever taken a road trip with animals?

- Have you ever gone on a vacation alone?

- Have you ever run out of gas?

- If you could move to any place in the world, where would it be?

- If you could travel anywhere in the world, where would you travel?

- If you could travel in any vehicle, which one would it be?

- If you had three things to wish for from a magic genie, what would they be?

- If you have a driver's license, how many times did it take you to pass the test?

- What are you the most afraid of on vacation?

- What do you want to get away from the most when you are on vacation?

- What foods smell bad to you?

- What item do you bring on ever trip with you away from home?

- What makes you sleepy?

- What song would you love to hear on the radio when you're cruising on the highway?

- What travel job would you want the least?

- What will you miss most while you are away from home?

- What is something you always wanted to try?

- What is the best road side attraction that you ever saw?

- What is the farthest distance you ever biked?

- What is the farthest distance you ever walked?

- What is the weirdest thing you needed to buy while on vacation?

- What is your favorite candy?

- What is your favorite color car?

- What is your favorite family vacation?

- What is your favorite food?

- What is your favorite gas station drink or food?

- What is your favorite license plate design?

- What is your favorite restaurant?

- What is your favorite smell?

- What is your favorite song?

- What is your favorite sound that nature makes?

- What is your favorite thing to bring home from a vacation?

- What is your favorite vacation with friends?

- What is your favorite way to relax?

- Where is the farthest place you ever traveled in a car?

- Where is the farthest place you ever went North, South, East and West?

- Where is your favorite place in the world?

- Who is your favorite singer?

- Who taught you how to drive?

- Who will you miss the most while you are away?

- Who if the first person you will contact when you get to your destination?

- Who brought you on your first vacation?

- Who likes to travel the most in your life?

- Would you rather be hot or cold?

- Would you rather drive above, below, or at the speed limited?

- Would you rather drive on a highway or a back road?

- Would you rather go on a train or a boat?

- Would you rather go to the beach or the woods?

TRAVEL BUCKET LIST

1.

2.

3.

4.

5.

6.

7.

8.

9.

10.

NOTES

Printed in Great Britain
by Amazon